WELCOME TO THE WORLD OF ANIMALS

Coyotes

Diane Swanson

Gareth Stevens Publishing
A WORLD ALMANAC EDUCATION GROUP COMPANY

199 8828

Please visit our web site at: www.garethstevens.com
For a free color catalog describing Gareth Stevens Publishing's list of high-quality books
and multimedia programs, call 1-800-542-2595 (USA) or 1-800-387-3178 (Canada).
Gareth Stevens Publishing's fax: (414) 332-3567.

The publishers acknowledge the support of the Canada Council for the Arts and the Cultural Services Branch of the Government of British Columbia in making this publication possible.

Library of Congress Cataloging-in-Publication Data

Swanson, Diane, 1944-
    [Welcome to the world of coyotes]
    Coyotes / by Diane Swanson. — North American ed.
        p. cm. — (Welcome to the world of animals)
    Includes index.
    Summary: Describes the physical characteristics, behavior, habitat, and life cycle
of the coyote, a type of wild dog that can reach speeds of forty miles per hour.
    ISBN 0-8368-3313-9 (lib. bdg.)
    1. Coyote—Juvenile literature. [1. Coyote.] I. Title.
QL737.C22S83   2002
599.77'25—dc21   2002021108

This edition first published in 2002 by
Gareth Stevens Publishing
A World Almanac Education Group Company
330 West Olive Street, Suite 100
Milwaukee, WI 53212 USA

This U.S. edition © 2002 by Gareth Stevens, Inc. Original edition © 2001 by Diane Swanson.
First published in 2001 by Whitecap Books, Vancouver/Toronto. Additional end matter © 2002
by Gareth Stevens, Inc.

Series editor: Patricia Lantier
Design: Katherine A. Goedheer
Cover design: Renee M. Bach

Cover photograph: Thomas Kitchin/firstlight.ca
Photo credits: Michael Quinton/firstlight.ca 4, 14, 18; Thomas Kitchin/firstlight.ca 6, 16; Mary
Clay/Dembinsky Photo Assoc. 8; Jim Battles/Dembinsky Photo Assoc. 10; Darrell Gulin/Dembinsky
Photo Assoc. 12; Mark Degner 20; Tim Christie/timchristie.com 22; Victoria Hurst/firstlight.ca 24;
Wayne Lynch 26, 28, 30

Printed in the United States of America

1 2 3 4 5 6 7 8 9 06 05 04 03 02

# Contents

World of Difference

Prairie wolf, brush wolf, little wolf — all are names people call the coyote. It's a wild dog with a bushy tail and a pointed face, but the coyote is no wolf.

Bigger than a fox and much smaller than a wolf, a good-sized coyote weighs about as much as a small dalmatian dog. Males are usually larger than females, and coyotes that live in cities — where there's plenty of food — grow heavier than those that live in the country.

The color of their coats varies from one coyote to another. The fur is often a mixture of gray, tan, and white, but it can

Even in winter, a coyote can sniff out whatever is around.

5

With its eyes focused on a mouse, a coyote leaps.

also include black. Some coyotes have coats that are mostly reddish or yellow-brown. During winter, they are normally lighter in color.

The coyote has keen senses that help it find food and escape enemies. A coyote's eyes can spot small movements among trees or in long grass. Its ears can hear the rustling of tiny feet beneath blankets of snow. And its nose can sniff a hiding rabbit — or an approaching mountain lion.

To chase down food or outrun danger, the coyote depends on a body built for speed. Its long legs are well designed for racing, and its tail provides balance. Held out to one side, it helps the coyote make sudden sharp turns while running. No wonder coyotes can live for eight years. Some even live to be ten years old or more.

COYOTE FEATS

Coyotes often amaze people. Here are some of the reasons why:

- **In short bursts, coyotes can reach speeds of 40 miles (65 kilometers) an hour.**

- **In some cities, coyotes have learned to follow dairy delivery trucks and drink milk left at doorways.**

- **During dry summer months, thirsty coyotes may dig to find water underground.**

7

Where in the World

Coyotes are critters of North and Central America — and nowhere else on Earth. At one time, they lived only in western parts of the continent, usually in woods and open country such as grasslands. But as people cleared dense forests for towns and farms, they created more space for coyotes — and more food, too.

Settlers also drove back two of the coyote's enemies — mountain lions and wolves. With fewer enemies around, coyotes increased in number and spread out.

Today there are many more coyotes than there once were, and they live

The dry, rocky lands of Arizona are home to some coyotes.

9

A coyote in a parking lot is no surprise in many cities.

throughout much of North and Central America. Coyotes have even moved into large cities. You might spot them on golf courses or in cemeteries and parks. They travel within cities by running along beaches, alleys, and railway tracks. They can also climb fences, or burrow beneath them, to get into backyards and gardens.

The space a coyote needs depends on the size of its family and the amount of food available. All that changes from season to season, year to year, and place to place.

Before female coyotes give birth, they snuggle into dens. But most of the time, coyotes just rest on the ground. They form beds by turning around and around, packing down the grass or snow. Many pet dogs — coyote cousins — do the same thing, even inside houses where there's often nothing to pack down.

FOLLOWING THEIR NOSES

Smells of food — including garbage and dead animals — attract coyotes. It was probably the odor of rotting seals that first lured coyotes from Nova Scotia to the island of Newfoundland in the 1980s. As they walked across the ice-covered water, they fed on the dead seals.

About one hundred years earlier, coyotes followed their noses northward. They ate garbage and dead mules left by gold miners heading for Alaska and the Yukon.

World Full of Food

You can't call coyotes fussy eaters. They feed on almost everything — grass, nuts, fruits, vegetables, eggs, insects, snakes, skunks, bats, birds, fish, and frogs. But mostly they eat rabbits, hares, and rodents such as mice and squirrels. Having a huge menu makes it possible for coyotes to live just about anywhere.

A coyote finds its meals quite easily — even underwater. It sticks its head into streams to grab fish and dives for crayfish.

Although a coyote can chase a fast-hopping rabbit or hare, it prefers not to waste energy. Belly to the ground, the

If there's food in a river, a coyote plunges right in.

Two coyotes work as a team to hunt bighorn sheep.

coyote often sneaks up close, then pounces on its prey.

Sometimes a coyote plays tricks to grab lunch. It might pretend to be dead until a crow comes close, then snatch the curious bird. The coyote might trail a badger to a den of ground squirrels and wait while the badger digs into the den.

When the squirrels try to escape from the badger, the coyote can grab one.

Coyotes also work in pairs to nab a meal. One coyote might scare a hare toward the waiting jaws of its partner. Or it might jump around to get the hare's attention while the partner sneaks up from behind.

When coyotes hunt a bigger animal, such as a deer, they work together as a team. They may take turns chasing it, so they can stay fresh while the deer wears out. When it drops down exhausted, the team moves in.

THREE CHEEPS FOR COYOTES!

Birds should be cheering — or cheeping — for coyotes. They sometimes feed on birds, but they also scare off or eat many other animals that hunt birds.

Around San Diego, California, scientists found that coyotes increased the number of birds by reducing the number of opossums, foxes, raccoons, and pet cats. The cats, alone, had been killing more than fifteen birds apiece every year. People who keep their pets indoors save birds from cats — and cats from coyotes.

World of Words

Expect rain when coyotes wail — or so Mexican folklore claims. Coyotes can't predict weather, but they do have plenty to say. Their barks, growls, yips, yelps, and howls are loaded with meaning. Parent coyotes, for instance, use sounds to call their young pups for dinner or to warn them to run and hide from danger. Pups make sounds to tell their parents they are hungry, in pain, or afraid.

Coyotes usually growl or huff to threaten something — or someone — that's close by. Barks or bark-howls make threats from a distance: "Go away!"

Nose to the sky, a coyote howls to its partner.

Not surprisingly, words of welcome sound much different. "Woo-oo-wow," says a coyote when it greets another. Or it might make a low-pitched whine, meaning the same thing. If the approaching coyote is more powerful, the greeter whines in a high-pitched voice instead. It also holds its tail low as it wags.

Using body language — narrowed eyes and a wrinkled snout — a coyote says "Scram!"

"Bark, bark, bark, h-o-w-l!" A lone coyote may call out, trying to contact others. Families seem to know if the message comes from one of their members or not. The coyotes answer by howling right back, which can help them get together again.

Sometimes howling seems to produce more howling. Coyotes not only answer calls from other coyotes, but they also respond to the howls of pet dogs and wolves — even to the wails of fire truck and ambulance sirens!

PECOS BILL

Nothing howls like a coyote, except Pecos Bill. At least, that's how the story goes. People still tell tall tales of a young pioneer boy who fell from a covered wagon near the Pecos River in Texas. He was rescued and raised by coyotes.

Pecos Bill learned to run, hunt — even talk — like a coyote. At night-time, he would join the others to bark, yip, and H-O-W-L at the moon. Some folks say Bill howled so long and so loud he sounded like a hundred coyotes.

New World

Coyote birthdays fall in springtime. Before the pups arrive, their parents search for nurseries — dens that are dry, hidden, and close to food and water.

Parent coyotes sometimes choose a cave or hollow log as a nursery. They might dig a burrow in a hillside or riverbank. More often, though, they take over an empty den that once belonged to a badger, skunk, or fox. The coyotes clean out the burrow. They might enlarge it and add an extra entrance, too.

Some female coyotes line their nurseries with layers of soft grass, leaves, or fur

A female coyote digs a den for a nursery.

Two tiny pups take a peek at their new world.

pulled from their bellies. Others don't bother providing any lining at all.

A coyote is usually born with three to five brothers and sisters. Sometimes there are as many as twelve pups — or more! Their birth size depends a lot on their numbers, but a new coyote weighs only about as much as a large potato.

Newborn pups are fuzzy, and their eyes are shut. They cuddle close to their mother for warmth and safety. For at least a week, the mother seldom leaves her pups. Her mate brings food to her and guards the den. Others in the family help, too, baby-sitting when the mother later heads off to hunt for food.

Father coyotes and baby-sitters also help the mother move her pups when necessary. For instance, she may change nurseries several times to avoid pests such as fleas.

SENSING THE WORLD

Inside an old skunk den, things smelled . . . well . . . a bit skunky. That didn't bother the coyote pups piled on top of one another. They had never been outside the den, never sniffed the fresh spring air.

All that was about to change, however. The pups were ten days old, and their eyelids were starting to flicker. Any minute, they would be able to see. Soon they would crawl to the den's entrance and — blink! sniff! — check out their world.

Small World

Little coyotes have big appetites. When they're only about two weeks old, they demand more than milk for dinner. They nibble around the lips of their parents to say, "Share your meals." The grown coyotes throw up some of the food that's in their stomachs. For the pups, vomit is a perfect meal — soft, warm, and nutritious.

As the pups grow, their parents start feeding them whole foods. They begin with small animals, such as insects and mice, and gradually add bigger animals. Later, dinners might include a ground squirrel, then a bird or rabbit.

A coyote starts howling when it's just a young pup.

This parent coyote would rather find food for its pup than play.

At first, the parents present the pups with dead animals. Soon they start bringing home live prey for the pups to help kill.

By the time coyote pups are eight or nine weeks old, they're ready to hunt with their parents. There is still a lot to learn. The pups must practice spotting, stalking, and nabbing animals such as grasshoppers. They also inspect the sky for ravens and vultures that have found food the pups might share.

Young coyotes try to avoid becoming meals themselves. They watch out for bobcats, eagles, wolverines, and other enemies. They also obey the sounds their parents use to warn, "Keep still. Be quiet."

After several more months, some of the pups may head out to find their own homes. Others stay with their parents, helping to care for next spring's pups.

HIGH-RISE COYOTE

Searching for food, a young coyote wandered through a passageway linking a riverbank with a tall building in Edmonton, Alberta. Cleaning staff spotted the coyote with its head stuck between the bars of a fifth-floor railing. It managed to squeeze its body through but fell to a balcony below. There, its head got stuck in another railing.

Police and wildlife officers worked to free the frightened coyote. Then they moved it outside the city.

Fun World

Coyote pups are wildly playful. They run. They leap. They twist and roll. It's not only great fun, it's good exercise, too. All these workouts help the pups grow well and develop strong muscles. Playing also wears the pups out, which helps them sleep well.

Coyotes like to play with toys. They sneak up on things such as stones, leaves, twigs, cones, bones, and feathers. They grab them and toss or bat them around. Pups even play with their food, flinging it up in the air before gulping it down.

Like people, coyotes sometimes play with others. They pretend to chase,

"Hey, let's play," a pup signals to its brother.

29

Chomp! One pup grabs another's snout — but it's all in fun.

wrestle, hunt — even kill — one another. It's part of the training they need for their later lives as grown coyotes. Playful pups exchange roles, switching back and forth from being "victims" to being "attackers." Parent coyotes sense that the pups are just playing and don't jump in to protect them.

Some coyote games seem like tests of strength. For instance, two pups might tug on the same stick or bone until one of them pulls it away. The winner — the stronger pup — may be the first to get fed by its parents.

When a pup is looking for a playmate, it often sends out signals. It squirms and rolls around on the ground. If no coyote responds, the pup might run around in circles, chasing its own tail.

COY TOYS

You have your toys, and coyotes have theirs. But in cities, they play with people's things, too. Young coyotes like to chase tennis balls and golf balls. They pounce on them and chew them up.

Even fuzzy slippers, leather sandals, and rubber tire scraps can become toys for coyotes. Two pups might grab the same one and p-u-l-l, starting a game of tug-of-war. An old rag yanked from a garbage can works just as well.

Glossary

burrow — (v) to dig a hole or tunnel in the ground; (n) an underground home for wild animals.

den — a home or shelter.

keen — sharp and sensitive; well developed.

lured — led away from or toward something by a scent, sound, or other attraction.

nab — to catch or grab quickly.

nurseries — places where eggs or young animals are cared for.

pounce — to suddenly swoop down or rush at something and grab it.

prey — animals that are hunted by other animals for food.

ravens — large, black birds that are related to crows.

snout — the long part of an animal's head containing the nose and mouth.

stalking — hunting by following very slowly and quietly.

wail — (v) to make a loud, long crying sound.

Index